T0333670

LEDBURY
PAST & PRESENT

RUTH SMITH

The History Press

The 'Butchers Row House'. Here it was situated behind Boots, which can be seen on the High Street, although today the building has been moved to a location in Church Lane. The premises are now home to Ledbury Museum. Until 1830 the building was positioned in the High Street near Lower Cross and was part of fifteen burgage houses and shops. (*Ledbury Museum*)

For Gran Gran

First published 2008

The History Press
The Mill, Brimscombe Port
Stroud, Gloucestershire, GL5 2QG
www.thehistorypress.co.uk

Reprinted 2009

© Ruth Smith, 2008

The right of Ruth Smith to be identified as the Author
of this work has been asserted in accordance with the
Copyrights, Designs and Patents Act 1988.

All rights reserved. No part of this book may be reprinted
or reproduced or utilised in any form or by any electronic,
mechanical or other means, now known or hereafter invented,
including photocopying and recording, or in any information
storage or retrieval system, without the permission in writing
from the Publishers.

British Library Cataloguing in Publication Data.
A catalogue record for this book is available from the British Library.

ISBN 978 07509 5054 1

Typesetting and origination by The History Press.
Printed in Great Britain

CONTENTS

ACKNOWLEDGEMENTS

There are many people whom I wish to thank, for without their help I would not have been able to compile and write this book at all. Many people have lent me their own personal photographs and collections and for this I am very grateful. To those who have kindly lent me photographs, thank you: Peter Judge; Sheila Hitchon; Robin Hill and Marianne Percival from Hereford Library; the staff at Ledbury Library; those at Ledbury Museum; Ann Bennion; Paul Dunthorne; Charles, Jenny and Bill Masefield; Benjamin Pardoe; John Wilesmith; Michelle and Royston Davies; Sharon Bingham; Chris Maulkin; Ann Thompson; Andrew Gurney; Bearnadette Kearney; and Martin Clarke.

Not only have I received help by borrowing physical photographs, but I have also had moral support from many people, so thank you to everyone for that as well. Also, thank you to my parents – to Mum for bringing me countless cups of coffee when I have been working upstairs at my desk, and to Dad, who wanted to be the 'manager' of this enterprise!

View from Dog Hill, looking down on Ledbury from its east side, in 1931. The church spire of St Michael and All Angels' can clearly be seen on the left. At the top of Church Lane the Tudor building – Church House – can also be spotted in the gap in the hedgerow. (*Alfred Watkins Collection, Hereford Library*)

INTRODUCTION

'The days that make us happy make us wise.'

John Masefield

It is perhaps the present name and size of Ledbury which has changed the most compared to the market town of 1120. The Domesday Book, compiled in 1086, recorded the town under the name of Liedeberge – in which the suffix *berg* derives from the Old English for walled town or borough. Ledbury has therefore been interpreted as a 'dwelling on the river Leadon'. The river runs about one mile west of the town centre. The town's population has increased from 3,058 in 1801 to 8,837 in 2001, according to the most recent census.

Not all of the changes which have occurred within the town are architectural: it lost some of its agricultural foundations when the Bye Street livestock market disappeared in 2000 and the ever-increasing volumes of traffic also do not enable animals to be driven through the town any longer.

Ledbury is able to boast many a famous person – including, of course, the poet laureate from the year 1930 until his death in 1967, John Masefield. Today the Masefield family still live in Ledbury, and run a solicitors firm on Worcester Road.

Other famous people from Ledbury include the poet Elizabeth Barrett-Browning, artist Conroy Maddox, cricketer Mary Duggan, footballer Steve Emery and the darts player Terry Jenkins.

I have lived on the outskirts of Ledbury all of my life, as has all of my family, and I have always enjoyed the town as a whole. In writing this book I have discovered a history which I was not previously aware of, so it has been a very enriching experience. I hope that this book brings to light a new perspective on the town and some of its more modern adaptations. I have taken all of the current day photographs myself, and within them I have attempted to maintain the same angle and position as to the old images. Some of Ledbury's most dramatic changes perhaps remind us how easily our heritage can be lost, and I feel we must strive to preserve it. I hope we will also try to keep intact the history Ledbury proudly presents to us as we walk its streets, use its buildings and speak to its people.

Ruth Smith, 2008

Bill Masefield, a close descendent of John Masefield, with his wife, Terri, who unfortunately passed away in early 2008. They are standing at the front of The Knapp, where John Masefield once lived.

ABOUT THE AUTHOR

Ruth Smith was born and brought up on a farm just outside Ledbury and enjoys living in this part of the country. She attended the Kings' School in Gloucester, where she completed her A-Levels in 2007. She is currently reading English Literature at Cardiff University. This is her first book.

1

THE WEATHER

Marcle Road in 1947. People clear away the snow in order to reach Robertson's Ledbury Preserves, which was founded in 1923. In March 2007 the site was bought out and current plans are for the largest cider mill in Western Europe to be built in a decade-long contract between Bulmers and the Q-Group. The venture would mill apples and other fruit to produce and package cider.

As a nation, one of our favourite pastimes would seem to be talking about the weather – Ledbury no more or less than anywhere else. It is often considered an 'ice-breaker' topic amongst new company, and so continuing this tradition, this first chapter is going to explore some of the notably extreme weather conditions which have occurred in this old market town. *(Peter Judge)*

The snow of 1947 meant that many people came to work together in helping to clear away the snow. Paused from shovelling and posing in the earlier photograph (above) are Harry Lewis and Doug Kington. The view is looking north up the Homend and the alley on the left between the two buildings is Belle Orchard. Today the layout of the street is still the same, as it curves to the right and the chimneys on the left-hand side are still in the same position. Where the sign for Cheltenham & Gloucester building society is on the right there used to be a grocer's called Bebbingtons, which sold animal feed in open sacks. It has been said that there would often be a cat found sleeping in one of the feed bags. *(Peter Judge)*

It seemed to snow everyday from January to March in 1947, so much so that on the top of British Camp in the Malvern Hills there was still snow in June. The winter of 1947 was marked as the snowiest since 1814. Pictured in these two photographs is the Homend. The men's clothes shop, Bradleys, was located on the left, where 'Ice Bytes', an internet café, now stands. *(Peter Judge)*

Mr Bill from Wellington Heath used to deliver milk from Eastnor, here in the Homend, in the snow. The casks can be seen on the sledge behind, and the height of the shovelled snow is put into perspective by the faces of two men in the background. The Boys' Church of England School was located in the Homend, and it was here that an unlucky janitor died of carbon monoxide poisoning during the 1947 snow. He was in the habit of sitting in the boiler room drinking cider; unfortunately the heavy snowfall blocked the chimney, stopping the boiler's deadly fumes from escaping. *(Peter Judge)*

The Homend in February 1947 (right) and as it is today (below). The house on the left is the former cottage hospital. Unfortunately this closed in 2002 and has remained empty and boarded up since. It has however been decided that the building will be refurbished and turned into six apartments plus managed workspace areas for local entrepreneurs. The building originally opened as a hospital in 1873 and was financed by Michael Biddulph in order to mark the coming of age of his eldest son, John. Ledbury's hospital exists today between Bye Street and New Street, where there used to be a livestock market. *(Peter Judge)*

People chat in the snow, 1947. The low building on the right is thought to have been the White Lion Inn during the late 1700s. At the turn of the nineteenth century this became the Swan Inn. Today this building is home to The Olive Tree, an Italian restaurant, which in 2007 extended its grounds into what used to be the Abbey Bakery. This bakery has relocated to a position in Bye Street. The iron bracket which held the sign for the Swan Inn above the window still serves the same purpose for The Olive Tree sign. *(Peter Judge)*

Church Lane in 1947 and 2008. Snow is being cleared in order to reach the fire station on the left, which is today located on Bye Street. With the size of fire engines today it would be difficult for them to quickly drive up and down Church Street, if at all. *(Peter Judge)*

The Ledbury Gas Company in the Homend has today been replaced by an opticians. It is possibly Gordon Smith clearing snow on the ladder (above). *(Peter Judge)*

Heavy snowing during the early months of 1947 blanketed the High Street. Both scenes reveal a busy town. Today, there are still a few trees on the pavement to the left, although not as many as in 1947. *(Ledbury Museum)*

The severe snow of 1982 created a perishing outside temperature of -15°C. The photograph shows Church Lane, with its picturesque cobbles hidden beneath the deep snow. The church is just a dark outline to the right of the buildings. *(Ledbury Museum)*

Right and below: Heavy flooding in June and July 2007 uprooted many of the original cobbles in Church Lane, causing some damage. Today Church Lane is home to council offices, Ledbury museum, the heritage centre, a chocolate shop, a café and the Prince of Wales public house. The heritage centre was formerly the King Edward VI Grammar School. Children were excused from school for numerous weeks during the period of snow in 1947. *(Revd Paul Dunthorne)*

Above and left: More of the flooding in 2007. Water gushes out of the gates from the churchyard and round the corner of the building, which is now the Ledbury Heritage Centre at the top of Church Lane. The flooding temporarily turned Church Lane into a river. Unfortunately, Ledbury Rugby Football Club flooded for a second time, causing considerable damage (the previous occurrence being in 1999). *(Revd Paul Dunthorne)*

2

BUILDINGS & STREETS

An aerial photograph of Ledbury taken in 1923. Both Bye Street and New Street have very narrow parts at the top of their respective streets which lead on to the High Street. The livestock market can be seen in the middle of the photograph leading off the two streets either side. The Market House is somewhat difficult to distinguish, although it can be seen to the right of the clock tower, which is named the Barrett-Browning Memorial Institute. The town is much less built up than today; the lower end of Bye Street still has the row of Tudor buildings rather than the fire station which now exists there, behind this can be seen the swimming pool, many flats and houses. The railway can also be seen in what was the original path of the canal. Neither of these exist today. *(Ledbury Library)*

The Market House in 1878. This is thought to date from 1633, although recently the dates have been somewhat disputed by historians. It was originally built as a grain store, although today it is used as a council meeting room. Parr's shop, which sold china and glass, can be seen to the right of the building. It is currently Ledbury News, which was formerly known as Balfour News. The Tudor building behind the Market House was altered in about 1890 and transformed into a curved Georgian building with brightly coloured brick. *(Benjamin Pardoe)*

The Market House in the early 1900s (above) and in 2008 (below). During the 1900s, Parr's shop was run by John Parr, who was also recorded as a seed dealer in a trade directory from the Victorian era. The shop to the right of Parr's was a grocer's which was run by Charles and Ellen Pedlingham whose family owned a number of stores in Ledbury, including a boot and shoe maker's, a confectioner's and a provision dealer's. As can be seen in the modern photograph, the shop façades and the Market House itself do not appear to have altered greatly in the last century. *(Benjamin Pardoe)*

The shop behind the Market House was the India and China Tea Company from 1902. Prior to that it was owned by John Ballard, and before that it was a grocer's. *(Peter Judge)*

Above and right: During the 1880s this grocer's was owned by John Ballard and run by Robert Edy. Behind this building there used to be a tallow candle factory and a large malthouse, which explains the name of a restaurant currently situated in Church Lane – The Malthouse. The building is currently occupied by Celebration, a craft shop formerly referred to as Ledbury Craft Centre. *(Ledbury Museum)*

The bottom of Church Lane in 1870. The centre building in the row of three on the left had a brick frontage from 1870 and in about 1890 the half timbered building on the far left was altered in the same way. This building was owned by William Smith, a shopkeeper and barber. *(Ledbury Museum)*

The building at the end of the row currently houses the Market House Café. The tourist information centre was housed in the building on the corner of the street on the left until early 2008, but is now Country Casuals, a clothing shop. The tourist information centre is now situated in the Master's House in St Katherine's car park behind the old almshouses.

Above and right: Church Lane, situated just behind the Market House, is still cobbled today, and many of the buildings here date back to the sixteenth and seventeenth centuries. This scene is probably one of the most photographed areas of Ledbury and indeed in Herefordshire. It is considered by many to be one of the most picturesque streets in Ledbury and is home to its council offices in the buildings on the immediate left. *(Peter Judge)*

Church House, also referred to as the Clerk's House, at the top of Church Lane. This lithograph was made in the early 1800s by the artist Thomas Ballard, who used to reside in the building next to the Barrett-Browning Memorial Institute, which is now occupied by Priory Cleaners. What is particularly interesting about the façade of Church House is its projecting room above the front door, allowing occupants to see both up and down Church Lane. *(Chris Maulkin)*

Pioneer photographer and antiquarian Alfred Watkins captured this image of Church House sometime during the early 1900s. Watkins was a highly cultured individual who, in 1921, first perceived the apparent arrangement of ancient features along straight lines, referred to as ley lines. However, not all archaeologists agree with his theories. Watkins travelled much around Herefordshire and came to know the area very well. A few of his images are used in this book although his more extensive collection is housed in Hereford Library. *(Alfred Watkins Collection, Hereford Library)*

The projecting frontage is still an original feature from when Church House was first built in around 1600.

Left and below: The building on the left used to be the King Edward VI Grammar School. However, it is believed that the school existed before King Edward's reign, in the 1500s. Mr Humphries, who maintained the site, had to educate four scholars for free as a form of rent. *(Ledbury Museum)*

Church House, looking at it head on. The barge boards attached to the four gables at the front are original features. The house is a fine example of a townhouse from the seventeenth century, built in an L-shape, on three floors and with a cellar below. The projecting porch is something which can also be found on the façade of the Talbot Inn. *(Ledbury Museum)*

Church Street, also known as Back Lane. In the nineteenth century this has seen some dramatic changes. These seventeenth-century cottages suffered tragic architectural developments when they were replaced by St Michael's flats which house the elderly. In 1974 the cottages were also demolished, and later, in 1983, the girls' school was destroyed. (*Alfred Watkins Collection, Hereford Library*)

Above and right: The gables of the girls' school can just be seen at the top of Church Street, beyond the Tudor buildings. Church Street meets Church Lane at its top end, and runs up from the Market House. *(Ledbury Museum)*

This is the west front of the St Michael and All Angels' Church, an uncommon angle as it is usually photographed from Church Lane. The earlier photograph (above) was evidently taken sometime in the late nineteenth century, as by 1900 the railings next to the church had been removed. Parts of the church are Norman, dating from 1180–1200. Since then some of it has been rebuilt, yet it retains original features, such as the door and some of the columns in the nave. It also bears some wounds and relics from the civil war. *(Alfred Watkins Collection, Hereford Library)*

Badsey's Walk and St Michael and All Angels' Church. The earlier photograph (above) is likely to have been taken in the late 1800s. The tower is actually detached from the main body of the church, an unusual design. The same paving can be seen in both images. *(Alfred Watkins Collection, Hereford Library)*

The Homend looking south. The absence of the Barrett-Browning Memorial Institute tells us that the earlier image (above) would have been photographed before 1894, the year in which work began on the clock tower. The bracket above the Swan Inn, on the right-hand side, tells us that George Webb was landlord (along with his wife Ann) during the 1880s. After a break of a few years at the end of the eighteenth century, after the closure of the White Lion Inn, the Barnes family took over, opening the Swan. When the Swan Inn closed it became the Swan Cycle Works. *(Alfred Watkins Collection, Hereford Library)*

Similar images, again looking south down the Homend; the earlier photograph dates from around 1870. Bank Crescent on the left-hand side, where the car is pulling out in the modern photograph, has not been constructed yet. The Horse Shoe Inn is the pub on the left. Cattle auctions were once held in this street, with the auctioneer standing at the top of the inn's steps, selling cattle to the buyers in the street. During such sales the pub was said to gain a lot of passing trade with buyers and sellers going in and out for a beverage. Today such an occurrence would not so easily happen due to the volume of traffic, and because the livestock market off Bye Street closed in 2000. *(Ledbury Museum)*

Left and below: Looking north up the Homend. The old houses on the right were replaced with Turner Court, a block of flats housing the elderly. The building was completed in the 1970s, at a similar time to the St Michael's flats in Church Street. The steps going up to these original properties were needed due to the height of the land behind them, so that the ground floor existed much higher than street level. This side of the street is still at a much higher level than the road and has steps from the road to the pavement. *(Alfred Watkins Collection, Hereford Library)*

Abbey House on the Homend in 1931 (above) and as it is today (right). It is situated next to the Horse Shoe Inn and has a projecting porch similar to Church House. Elizabethan in style, it is thought to date back to around 1600, and was likely to have been built at the same time as Church House, the second part of the Feathers Hotel and both the Talbot Inn and the Steppes in New Street. *(Alfred Watkins Collection, Hereford Library)*

The Barrett-Browning Memorial Institute was built in order to commemorate the poet Elizabeth Barrett-Browning. In 1890 a meeting was held to discuss the idea, and six years later it was officially opened. The building led to the demolition of shops, stables and the tannery on the corner of the Homend and Bye Street. The shops seen in this rare photograph from around 1890 consist of Thomas Morgan, boot and shoemaker, Mr Johnson's hairdressers and tobacconists in the middle (the proprietor can be seen standing outside in a white apron), and Gibbs & Son stationery shop and printers on the left. *(Ledbury Museum)*

The Barrett-Browning Memorial Institute had at first been proposed to be built adjacent to the Market House in the town centre, yet the volume of traffic nowadays may have made such a decision an unforgiving one. The total cost of the building amounted to £2,330. From 1938 the institute has housed the public library, but the future of this is uncertain due to the need for disabled access. *(Ledbury Museum)*

The High Street looking north. The earlier photograph (above) dates from the 1930s, while the modern photograph (below) was taken in 2008. *(Ledbury Museum)*

The High Street, *c.* 1890. The volume of traffic is much less than today and there is no sign yet of the motor car. The rendering here still covers the buildings on the left-hand side. Where there was once Charles W. Stephenson's ironmonger's there is now a delicatessen, café and kitchen shop. On the right used to be Tilley's shop (its cart can be seen in front) which was destroyed by a car in 1970. *(Ledbury Museum)*

At the top of Bye Street in the early twenty-first century. These buildings were replaced with more modern looking shops and office space. The building in the middle was a removal business which would take in old furniture. *(Benjamin Pardoe)*

The same buildings during reconstruction (above) and in their present state in 2008 (below). Clubsport is a family owned business with several other branches in Herefordshire and nearby counties. A familiar face around Ledbury, Steve Onions of the former Ledbury Sports, which used to exist further down the other side of the street, has merged his business with Clubsport. *(Benjamin Pardoe)*

Bye Street, *c.* 1900. The street appears to be extraordinarily quiet compared with the amount of traffic today. At one time Bye Street had buildings down the middle, which can be seen on the left in this photograph, but these have since gone, making way for properties on Masefield Close and Ledbury fire and ambulance station (which moved from the bottom of Church Street). The Bye Street Market, which once took place in the area on the right, is now Ledbury Community Hospital. (*Alfred Watkins Collection, Hereford Library*)

Bye Street in 1981 (above) and 2008 (below). *(Ledbury Museum)*

Above: This row of cottages used to be adjacent to the Brewery Inn, opposite the old cattle market off Bye Street, but was demolished to make way for the fire and ambulance station. *Below:* The market was replaced by the community hospital at the beginning of this century. Behind the buildings is Ledbury Swimming Pool, whose white triangular roofs can just be seen in the background. *(Ledbury Museum)*

New Street in the late 1800s (above) and the same scene in 2008 (below). The buildings on the right-hand side and the Steppes on the left were still rendered. The Talbot Inn, sometimes referred to as Old Talbot or even Ye Olde Talbot, on the right was also still covered. At the time of this photograph C. Wetson was the landlord, which was from 1881 to 1890. The Vine Tap pub can also be seen on the right-hand side, which is currently a Chinese take away. *(Alfred Watkins Collection, Hereford Library)*

The Top Cross on the corner between New Street and the Southend, looking east from the Worcester road in 1890. Hampton's sold shoes priced between 5s 9d and 10s 6d. Some have thought this building to originally have been the centre of Ledbury and possibly even a market house. *(Ledbury Museum)*

Views of the Top Cross in 1965 (above) and 2008 (below). By 1965 the rendering had come off this corner building. At that time the traffic had priority across the Ross to Malvern road, rather than over the Hereford to Gloucester road as is today's situation. Today this building is a wedding shop. *(Ledbury Museum)*

Above and below: This building is Ledbury Park which, until 1829, was known as the New House. It originates from around 1595 and used to be the home of the Biddulphs. Their family lived at Ledbury Park for more than 250 years, having acquired the building through marriage in around 1680. The close set timber on the exterior walls of the house denoted wealth, because the wood was expensive. This particular postcard was sent on 19 July 1927. To the far left, beyond the domed turret, the building was extended during the 1800s. *(Michelle and Royston Davies)*

Garden Front, The Park, Ledbury. No. 1.

Two views of Ledbury Park in about 1905 (above) and 2008 (below). The wall on the left is the one which faces onto the Southend and conceals its grounds. The building once acted as Prince Rupert's headquarters in the English Civil War and also housed Queen Victoria on a visit. For some time it used to be the residence of H.J. Chapman stationers and printers. Today it is divided up into flats. *(Michelle and Royston Davies)*

Worcester Road in 1912 (above) and 2008 (below). The building on the left is Masefield's solicitors, which has been practicing since about 1830. The road was originally referred to as Horse Lane, probably because of the number of horse-drawn carriages which used to travel along it to Worcester. Also on the left was a toll house, which was demolished in 1953. By the following year this site was made ready for Ledbury police station, which is still located on these premises. On the right there used to be an orchard, but this has now been replaced by a housing estate. *(Ledbury Museum and Ledbury Library)*

The Southend in January 1908. This is one of the original medieval streets in Ledbury, gaining the name from its position at the southern end of town. *(Peter Judge)*

Many of the town's properties date from the Georgian era, including the impressive Gloucester House on the left with the old toll house at the end. John Masefield Senior School is located further down the road on the left.

This sundial ,originating from 1783, is sited on the wall of Bowling Green Cottage, on the east side of the Southend, opposite the toll house. *(Ledbury Museum)*

The toll house at the junction of Mabel's Furlong and the Southend, next to Gloucester House, in the 1980s. It would appear that the building is the same as today, yet it was found that it needed extensive repairs on the wall which protected its original state from view. *(Ledbury Museum)*

The toll house in the process of being completely demolished and then rebuilt, February 1982. *(Ledbury Museum)*

In 2008 the toll house is in good condition and acts as a tiny cottage. During the 1700s and early 1800s there were nine toll stations leading out from Ledbury's major roads which levied traffic.

3

TRANSPORT

Photographer Alfred Watkins captured this image on his two-day canoe trip down the entire length of the Hereford and Gloucester canal, *c.* 1880–1. The building of the canal began during the 1790s, a popular era for such things, yet was not completed until 1845. The canal from Ledbury to Gloucester was open by 1798, but the entire system had closed by 1885. It was only when Alfred Watkins heard that the canal was due to close that he and a friend, Ted George, whose father was involved in a timber business at the canal wharf in Hereford, decided to embark on their canoe journey. *(Alfred Watkins Collection, Hereford Library)*

A postcard of Ledbury station dating back to 1917 (above), and the station today (below). The station buildings were modernised in the 1960s. Today there is simply a small station building. In the modern-day image one can see that the road is more vehicle friendly. In the distance is a billboard, showing how advertising continues in our lives today. *(Ledbury Museum)*

The station yard entrance in the early twentieth century (above) and today (below). Staff of the Tilley business pause for a photograph in the midst of pinning up advertisements in 1911. This was a perfect place for posters due to the constant use of the station. Even today this wall alerts people to businesses located up the road. The cart on the right survived until 1970, when it was destroyed by a car. The vehicle on the left is thought to be either a Standard or Star, *c.* 1910. Its back seat passenger is Mr Luke Tilley, who set up the Tilley business in Ledbury. His brother, John Tilley, was a keen photographer and took many pictures which still exist today. The bike in the centre has fittings for an engine, meaning that it was probably a Warner, *c.* 1904. *(Ledbury Museum)*

The west section of the tunnel at Ledbury station, 1884. The grounds of the canal were leased to the Great Western and West Midland railways after it closed in 1862, with a view to convert it into a railway. The path of the canal had followed the valley of the Leadon in order to link the River Wye to the Severn. It had a diversion at Newent to go to the collieries, which meant that a huge tunnel was constructed at Oxenhall. This was never a success, partly as the coal was of poor quality, so this section of the canal fell into disuse. For Ledbury in the early 1800s the canal was a great benefit economically, but its cost had escalated hugely and it was never fully completed. The wharf was located at the end of New Street. When the railway from Hereford to Worcester opened in 1861, coal merchants began to use its services rather than those offered by the canal. In 1885 the Gloucester to Ledbury railway opened on the line of the canal. It served passengers for seventy-four years, until July 1959, after which it continued to operate for freight traffic only for a further five years. Finally, in May 1964, the Ledbury to Gloucester line closed fully, leaving just bridges and other features as reminders of what once was. Some may suggest that just as the canal was unable to compete with the prospect of trains, some of these trains were also unable to cope with the prospect of the motor car. In Ledbury therefore, transport has progressed from water to rail to land, now with the Ledbury bypass, Leadon Way, built in 1969. *(Alfred Watkins Collection, Hereford Library)*

The station in about 1906 (above) and 2008 (below). In 1906 the Ledbury to Gloucester line was still open and a train is just pulling in on the left. Simultaneously a train is leaving the station bound for Worcester. The station yard is also busy, where horses are loaded up to carry wares. In 2008 a train has just arrived having come through the tunnel. *(Alfred Watkins Collection, Hereford Library)*

The viaduct whilst still under construction, *c.* 1861. The workmen had a miniature railway which was used to bring materials back and forth, which can be seen just behind the fence. The viaduct was made from 5,000,000 bricks, which were made on the site. The whole bridge in total made up thirty-one arches, each 60ft high. *(Ledbury Library)*

It has been suggested that the Leadon Way may be extended beneath the viaduct in order to make the bypass longer to meet the Bromyard road, but it is hoped by many that this will not occur and the viaduct will remain set away from traffic and the fields will not be destroyed by such developments. *(Ledbury Library)*

The viaduct was nearly completed by June 1861. The figure in the top hat on the left of the small railway is thought to be Robert Ballard, who engineered the viaduct and was related to Stephen Ballard, who was a boat builder and clerk of the canal company, very much involved with the Hereford to Gloucester canal. *(Ledbury Library)*

The viaduct, pictured nearing completion in 1861 (above), and in 2008 (below) with a train going to Hereford. *(Ledbury Library)*

A picturesque image of the viaduct from the meadows looking east towards Ledbury. A train with six coaches is crossing the bridge. The viaduct leads in a north-westerly direction out of Ledbury to Hereford. *(Ledbury Library)*

Above: People gather round to see off the last passenger train leaving Dymock station to go to Ledbury on 11 July 1959. *Below*: Today all that is left is a bridge and the original station platform which can just about be distinguished amongst the grass. There is a children's play area and a housing estate in the vicinity. *(Peter Judge)*

Road works in the Homend, *c.* 1925. This was perhaps when the cobbles were being taken up. The inn on the right (where a sign is hanging) was the Plough at no. 74, which closed in the 1990s. Today this exists as an Indian restaurant. *(Peter Judge)*

Above and below: In early 2008 road works took hold of Ledbury's streets. They were supposed to be in place from January until May, but were finished early. This meant that the town was temporarily forced to operate on a one-way system. The reason for the escapade was to allow Welsh Water to work beneath the tarmac.

The High Street in 1915 (above) and 2008 (below). The horse-drawn carriage on the right approaching the Top Cross was owned by the Royal Oak Hotel in the Southend, which used to ferry guests to and from the station. As can be seen by the sign, the Feathers Hotel on the left used to offer 'motor cars for hire' at its garage. The street today is home to much more traffic, both cars and buses. A postman's cart is on the left delivering mail. *(Ledbury Museum)*

The High Street in 1900 (right) and 2008 (below). At the time the earlier photograph was taken the Feathers' frontage was still rendered. During the nineteenth century the Feathers Hotel played host to the half-yearly meeting for the administrators of the Herefordshire and Gloucestershire Canal Co. who, during the early 1800s, were still trying to finish the development. The horse-drawn cart on the right belonged to the Vine Tap Inn, which was located in New Street. In the modern photograph a steam engine travels northwards down the High Street. *(Ledbury Museum)*

One way of travelling around, both for children and adults alike was of course via horse and cart. Here two children are giving their donkey water outside St Katherine's almshouses. These were part of the original St Katherine's Hospital built in the 1800s. *(Peter Judge)*

The railings, seen here in 2008, are not the original ones, which were removed during the Second World War. The pump on the trough has also gone. The trough itself is now set back against the railings rather than situated on the roadside, and the cobbles have been replaced with paving stones.

4

EVERYDAY LIFE

On 6 December 2000 the last livestock market took place in Ledbury, on the site where the Community Hospital now stands. The market was held weekly, selling animals and other local and seasonal produce. The two gentlemen on the left engaged in conversation are farmers Frank Bennion (left) and Charlie Churchill (right), who was formerly part of Churchill's Butcher's operating on the High Street. (*Ann Bennion*)

The market located between Bye Street and New Street in the early 1900s (above), and the present-day site (below). The auctioneers were Lomas & Anthony, who were previously W. Manton & Co. for whom there is still a sign on the left. The market would have held over 1,000 animals and was erected in 1887 in order to get livestock away from the High Street, which was proving to be less than hygienic. *(Ledbury Library; Benjamin Pardoe)*

Above and below: The Ledbury Community Hospital was built in 2001 on the site of the livestock market, and covers an area of 4,500 sq.m. It contains a variety of facilities, including doctors, dentists, an accident and emergency unit and a nursing home. *(Benjamin Pardoe)*

Cattle and sheep would regularly be driven through the High Street, even when the market had moved to its new site off Bye Street. Here, in 1908, they are making their way up Worcester Road. Today it is unlikely one would see livestock coming through the town. *(Ledbury Museum; Peter Judge)*

Above: In 1912 sheep are being driven up the Worcester Road. *Below*: In 2008 the traffic would restrict such movements; instead animals are transported in lorries and trailers. *(Ledbury Library)*

Pens on the High Street outside the Market House would have held sheep and pigs on the livestock market day, which was every second Tuesday of the month. Horses and cattle would be held in the Homend. This was here until 1887, when the Ledbury Markets & Fairs Co. Ltd and the market on Bye Street were set up in order to get animals away from the High Street. *(Ledbury Museum)*

Sheep and cattle being driven down the Homend, *c.* 1900 (above) and the same scene today (below). The shop on the left was William Harris's ironmongery, selling bags, baskets, pots and pans. The inn to the right of the railings was the White Horse Inn, a beer house which closed in 1930. Set back off the road behind the railings is a Baptist church, which is still there today. *(Ledbury Museum)*

The Lower Cross in the early 1900s, where a young herd of calves are being driven northwards up the Homend, presumably to a local farm. *(Ledbury Museum)*

Above and below: By 1935 the horse-drawn carts have been replaced by motor cars, one of which is overtaking the Herefordshire oxen with their cart at Lower Cross. The arrival of lorries in the 1930s lead to a decline in livestock being herded through the streets. The New Inn can be seen on the left, this pub was originally The Crown, sometimes called the Old Crown. The New Inn closed in the 1970s, and has since been converted into shops which collectively are referred to as the Homend Mews. *(Ledbury Museum)*

A busy market in 1900 (above). The stalls in the 2008 photograph (below) were part of *Marche de France*, the French market which had come from Normandy. Among the products available were cheeses, sausages, olives, garlic, breads, wines and cakes. Between Friday 4 and Sunday 6 April the market set up in Ledbury, Hereford and Bromyard. *(Ledbury Museum)*

Two views from beneath the Market House. The cobbles on the High Street can clearly be seen, which used to cover all of the pavements in Ledbury. The stones and pebbles would have been tapped into gravel beneath. The French market can again be seen (below), with many people surveying the produce. *(Alfred Watkins Collection, Hereford Library)*

A market scene. In the late 1800s the Barrett-Browning Memorial Institute has not yet been built and we can see the buildings which existed there previously. The tannery was thought to have been built in around 1600. The lamp fixed onto the corner of the Market House was provided as part of an initiative by Hereford Council to light Ledbury. The gas it used came from the Ledbury Gas, Coal & Coke Ltd, which was located in New Street. (*Alfred Watkins Collection, Hereford Library*)

The market in the early 1900s (above), and the French market from Normandy selling produce in April 2008 (below). *(Peter Judge)*

Above and opposite: Gypsies at the top of the Southend, outside Ledbury Park, *c.* 1930. Herefordshire used to be an attractive spot for gypsies because of the seasonal work which farms could offer. It would appear that today there are fewer road travellers, partly because the work is sparser due to farmers having more technical machinery and the increased use of foreign labour. Today the town does still see gypsies travelling through, but due to an increase in traffic it would be unlikely that they could park for very long in this now traffic-light controlled spot. *(Alfred Watkins Collection, Hereford Library)*

Above and below: During the hop-picking season, generally in September, Ledbury would see the arrival of many people who came to work in hop yards. Often whole families, who had travelled usually via train from places such as South Wales or the Black Country, would work picking the hops and use it as a chance to escape to the country. Locals would also work and sometimes a noticeable contrast was distinguishable between those who had travelled and those who lived nearby who had dressed up in smart hats. Here, in the early 1900s pickers are getting the hops from the poles on which they were grown and then putting them in the crib. The family gathered around the crib is the Betteridge family of Marley Hall, picking in 1908, near Bosbury. *(Ledbury Museum)*

Local hops producing beer, and apples producing cider give a good enough reason for the number of pubs that Ledbury has been home to over the years. One of these pubs includes the Old Talbot Inn, pictured here in the 1880s before the rendering was removed (right), and in its present state in 2008 (below). The Talbot is one of the few pubs to contain a complete list of all of its landlords, dating back to the late 1700s. It was built in 1596 and was a coaching inn similar to the Feathers. *(Alfred Watkins Collection, Hereford Library)*

The Feathers Hotel was originally referred to as the Plume of Feathers. This name was adopted in order to acknowledge loyalty to the Crown – the title refers to the three ostrich feathers which were once adopted as a crest by Edward, the Black Prince. The coach waiting outside in 1890 was used to take guests to and from the train station. The Feathers used to be a posting house, a four-horse Royal Mail carriage would arrive at approximately 10 a.m. having come from London via Cheltenham to collect and deliver letters. The rendering concealing the timber behind was removed in about 1908. There was also a room in the building which acted as the Corn Exchange. *(Ledbury Museum)*

The motor car has become a much more prominent feature by the time this 1900s photograph was taken. Today the Feathers is still a thriving hotel and pub providing accommodation, food and drink. *(Peter Judge)*

A distinctive characteristic amongst these views of the Brewery Inn in Bye Street is the spire of the church standing proudly in the distance. Even though the inn itself looks exactly the same in all of the images the street itself is a very much changed scene. The row of old houses to the right disappeared, as did those beyond the inn on the left, where the fire and ambulance stations now stand. Here we can see the Brewery Inn in 1890 (left) and again in 1910 (below). *(Ledbury Museum)*

The Brewery Inn, Bye Street, in 1981 (right) and 2008 (below). It is located very close to where both the canal and the railway used to run, whose paths used to go beneath a bridge which exists further down, on the aptly-named Bridge Street. In the 1881 census the pub was called The Brewery, although some believe that before this it was called the Bridge Inn and also the Canal Inn. *(Ledbury Museum)*

Above and below: The Seven Stars pub suffered a disastrous fire in 2001, which fire-fighters believed was the largest they have had to conquer in Ledbury's memory. The start of the fire was somewhat ambiguous, but the article recording the incident in the *Hereford Times* stated that 'a Ledbury woman ... of the Homend ... was remanded in custody to appear at Worcester Crown Court ... charged with arson.' A year later, in July 2002, the landlady was cleared of these same charges. (*Benjamin Pardoe*)

Above and below: A restoration programme had begun on the Seven Stars by October 2001. The adjoining buildings were also affected and had to be repaired. Today the pub looks very similar to its original appearance, apart from the colour of the paintwork. *(Benjamin Pardoe)*

Above and below: The New Inn, a few buildings down from the Seven Stars, closed in the mid-1970s and now exists as shops and the area is referred to as the Homend Mews. Pictured here in the early twentieth century, the New Inn served as a hostelry and posting station. Today the front of the building is rendered. *(Ledbury Museum)*

Above and right: The Prince of Wales in Church Lane. The past and present-day landlords stand outside – in early 1942 this was George Carter, and in 2008 Les Smith, (since July 2003). The building, dating from the late 1500s, is fortunate in that it can also be accessed from Church Street. During the building of the railway, landlords John and Eliza Tomkins had two lodgers who were labourers on the railway. Opposite the back of the Prince of Wales's entrance used to be the White Hart Inn, which closed in 2001. *(Andrew Gurney)*

Jones's bookseller and stationer in 1896. The store relocated from no. 10 the Homend, to no. 20 the Homend, where today there exists a confectioner's called The Chocolate Box, selling chocolates, sweets and gift cards. *(Ledbury Museum)*

William Madders & Son's grocer's shop at the top of the Homend. The figure standing on the left was 'old' Mr Madders. The window on the right used to display meats and dairy products, and the window on the left cleaning equipment. In the 1970s a lorry smashed into the façade of the building and it was rebuilt. Today it is a specialist gun shop. *(Ledbury Library)*

This was Tilley's shop at no.16 on the High Street. The family was a very important and prominent one in town. Luke Tilley, one of five brothers, originally came to Ledbury in 1869 to start their business as a stationers and printers. The family also created a library which lasted until the 1960s. The *Tilley's Almanac* – a phone directory – is still sporadically produced today but much of its trade has now decreased. The shop is now a gift shop called Nice Things. They also used to occupy the building next door which is now a female clothing shop. *(Ledbury Library)*

This was S.S. Gallop's shop, also a stationer, at the point of transfer to the Tilley family. The ladies with the bikes (below) are also presumably part of the Tilley empire – delivering newspapers. However, we do not know who they were or where they came from. *(Ledbury Library)*

This was the fishmongers and poultry suppliers McDonald & Co., located adjacent to the Feathers Hotel. They also sold game and fruit. Today matters of hygiene would disallow the meat to be hung outside. The store would travel to nearby villages to deliver their produce. Today an interior design and fashion accessory shop called Wyebridge Interiors exists in its place. *(Ledbury Library)*

5

ROYAL OCCASIONS

A crowd celebrates Queen Victoria's Diamond Jubilee in 1897. A table is laid out for people to sit down and eat at the festivities. *(Ledbury Museum)*

Looking south down the Homend. A street party celebrates Queen Victoria's Golden Jubilee in June 1887. A huge table is laid out for people to sit down and eat at the festivities. *(Ledbury Museum)*

Looking north up the Homend for the Golden Jubilee. The lady on the right dressed in black and wearing the bonnet is allegedly John Masefield's 'widow of Bye Street', as she is called in one of his poems. *(Ledbury Museum)*

June 1887: crowds pour outside for a street party to celebrate Queen Victoria's Golden Jubilee. People have dressed up in their Sunday best, and the masses stretch right up the Homend. *(Ledbury Museum)*

Lower Cross, adjacent to the Market House, 23 June 1960. Crowds gather to welcome Her Majesty the Queen Mother on her visit to Ledbury. *(Charles and Jenny Masefield)*

To Her Majesty's far left is the Chairman of Ledbury Urban District Council, Mr Harold Brown, and to her immediate left is the Lord Lieutenant of Herefordshire, James Thomas, 1st Viscount Cilcennin. *(Charles and Jenny Masefield)*

Her Majesty is presented with flowers by a young girl. *(Charles and Jenny Masefield)*

Above and below: In July 2003 Her Majesty Queen Elizabeth II visited Ledbury, coming to Harling Court, a sheltered accommodation. Crowds came to watch and support her as she travelled up the road and entered the building.

On Queen Elizabeth II's Coronation Day, 2 June 1953, people across the country celebrated on the streets. Ledbury was no exception, and next to the Market House a hog was roasted on a spit. *(Ann Bennion)*

6

WAR YEARS

Speeches on Empire Day, also known as
Commonwealth Day, May 1916. Both the young
and old gathered round the raised flag to listen
and show patriotism towards the British Empire.
(Ledbury Library)

During the First World War the Red Cross raised money in Herefordshire by travelling around with the Bosbury Red Cross donkey, which was owned by Mr Lane of Old Court Farm. The funds generated were painted onto the back of the cart, including £313 earned in Ledbury. Often, two of Mr Lane's daughters, who were nurses, would travel in the cart. *(Ledbury Library)*

This was Mr William Lewis, commonly referred to as 'Old Bill', renowned in Ledbury and also Herefordshire for fund raising for various charities. In fact, he was the official collector for Ledbury Cottage Hospital and raised several hundred pounds in his days as a charity collector. He used to dress up in a silk hat and a spectacular suit. *(Ledbury Library)*

Nearly eighty men were called up from Ledbury to fight in the First World War in August 1914. The soldiers marched through town, amidst supporting crowds, flags and posters, to the station where they departed to Hereford in order to change trains to travel to Pembroke Dock. *(Ledbury Library)*

The cavalry proceeding towards the Top Cross. *(Ledbury Library)*

Above: Ledbury Home Guard on parade in 1943. During the Second World War there was a prisoner of war camp where the Deep Park housing estate now stands. The prisoners often became friends with those in the community and would not only perform tasks such as cleaning out rivers and ditches, but they also built a theatre in the camp where a dramatic society began, and where school plays came to be held. *(Ledbury Museum)*

Left: The war memorial remembering Ledbury's victims from the First World War, referred to as 'The Great European War', and the Second World War stands in the High Street. The roll of honour lists eighty names from the First World War and forty-three from the Second World War. The memorial was erected in December 1920, and costs came to £600. An unveiling and dedication ceremony was held, with crowds of people and surviving ex-servicemen honouring those who had sacrificed their lives.

7

SPORTS & EVENTS

A procession on the High Street, part of the Hospital Sunday Church Parade, 19 July 1908.
The display started near the railway station and progressed to Gloucester House in the Southend,
then turned around and came back through the town, via Woodleigh Road and Bridge Street to
the church for a service. The aim of the parade was to raise money for the cottage hospital in the
Homend, for which £24 was made at the procession and £6 at the service. *(Ledbury Library)*

In June 1911 the Herefordshire and Worcestershire Show took place for three days at Hazel Farm, just outside Ledbury. The farm has since been sold and divided up into houses. A farming store, Countrywide, was also built on some of its land. *(Ledbury Museum)*

A procession of local businessmen and public figures walk down New Street on their way to the show. The banner displays the arms of the city of Hereford. The building on the left is the Steppes, built in about 1600, which has a Georgian doorway and was once a merchant's townhouse. *(Ledbury Library)*

Above and below: Ledbury Street Carnival is an annual event which takes place every August Bank Holiday. In the 1980s the street also had fairground rides, and in 2007 the crowds surge after the last of the floats have passed. The floats progress from Ledbury Rugby Club and come up new street, turning left at the Top Cross and making their way down the High Street. (*Sharon Bingham*)

A carnival group in 1926 or 1927 (above). Some of the men are Morris dancers, a tradition which continues across Herefordshire to this day. The carnival stopped for a period of years during the 1900s and began again in 1975. A group of Morris men also gather in Church Lane outside the Prince of Wales pub in 1997 (below). *(Ledbury Museum; Wikipedia)*

Above: On Boxing Day 2007 a group of Morris men performed outside the Market House after the Ledbury Hunt had passed through the town.

Right: A Morris man dressed up for an August Bank Holiday carnival in the 1980s. *(Sharon Bingham)*

Ledbury Hunt kennels, early 1900s. The hounds were kept here until 1938 when the kennels relocated to Bromesberrow. The kennels were built in 1868 and were situated just off the Bromyard Road adjacent to the train station. The Ledbury Hunt, according to the original book of minutes, can be traced back as far as 1846 when a committee was made. Hounds are also known to have been hunting in this area for over 300 years. The Ledbury Hunt covers the Herefordshire and Gloucestershire borders. Since the 2004 hunting ban, Ledbury Hunt continues to meet and operate within the limitations of the law. *(Ledbury Library)*

Ledbury Hunt continues to meet every Boxing Day, and crowds gather to greet and support those involved. *Below*: The mass of riders follow the hounds passing Southwards down the High Street in 2007. *(Ledbury Library)*

Above: The hunt proceeding southwards down the High Street next to the Market House during the late 1960s on Boxing Day. The rider on the white horse is Nimrod Champion, the huntsman. *Below*: In 2007 the town crier, William Turberfield, commonly known as Bill, heads the procession. Bill received the position of town crier after beating fellow applicants in a shouting audition in the Walled Garden. In both photographs the horses have turned around at Lower Cross in order to make the journey back towards the Top Cross. *(Sheila Hitchon)*

Ledbury Hunt on Boxing Day during the 1990s, proceeding south towards Lower Cross from the Homend. *(Ann Thompson)*

The hunt beginning the procession through the town, as the party head north down the High Street on a Boxing Day in the late 1960s. The rider is Nimrod Champion. The steak bar in the background was then called the Hereford Bull, after being simply called The Bull. It is now the Retreat, a pub. Fosters, two shops to the right, is now Boots. *(Sheila Hitchon)*

A lawn meet at Netherton Farm in Eastnor, Wednesday 14 January 1970. From left to right are Mr Nimrod Champion, the huntsman; Mr and Mrs B. Blandford, standing amongst the hounds; Bunty Blandford; Mr A. Smith-Maxwell; Mrs J. Oram; Captain R. Hoare and Mr E.F. Bensley – all of whom were joint masters for different periods of time during the 1960s and '70s; and finally those in front are gamekeepers, Mr P. Cox and Mr T. Pearce. Nimrod Champion became the huntsman for the Ledbury Hunt in 1949 and continued to be so for thirty-four seasons until his death in 1983, aged fifty-nine. Nimrod was one of the most respected huntsmen in the country having followed the role of his father Bob, maintaining Ledbury Hunt's reputation of being one of the best two-day-a-week packs in the country. Nimrod and his three brothers were the fourth generation of his family to hunt. His father had been invited to choose one of his four sons to become huntsman. Nimrod was the youngest and took on the position after serving as a pilot in the Second World War. *(Sheila Hitchon)*

A lawn meet at the Burtons in Wellington Heath, New Year's Day 1973. On horseback are Mr Champion and Mr Pollack. *(Sheila Hitchon)*

Nick Ross, the Ledbury Hunt Falconer, in 2006. Nick came to the Ledbury Hunt in August 2005 and is believed to be the only falconer who rides throughout the duration of the hunt with a falcon. For the first four months Nick walked with the hunt, then in January 2006 he began to ride as well, even jumping all of the fences.

Two young women, Linda Rea with Cusop Queen and her sister Sheila Rea with Mealy Jay, both arrive for the Boxing Day Ledbury Hunt meet in December 1970. Behind them the rider is Francis Daniels, who was a part-time trainer of race horses. *(Sheila Hitchon)*

The same hunt meet is leaving the town after having progressed up the High Street. Sheila Rea rides Mealy Jay, the white horse, and her sister Linda is ahead on Cusop Queen. *(Sheila Hitchon)*

The Boxing Day meet of 1972 leaves town. The rider on the horse on the far left is Patt Gardiner from Pixley and the rider on the horse next to him is Tim Houlbrooke. The rider on the front white horse is Juliet Whatley, and the rider to the left and slightly ahead is Sheila Rea. *(Sheila Hitchon)*

Above: Part of the Ledbury Hunt, New Year's Day 1973, at the Burtons in Wellington Heath. Those gathered for a break during the Ledbury Hunt are Miss Ann Morris with Nutty; Linda Rea with Mealy Jay; Sheila Rea with Cusop Queen; Victoria Younghusband with Prince; and Mr Andrew Younghusband with a grey. *(Sheila Hitchon)*

Right: The Top Cross, Boxing Day 2006. On horseback are mother and son, Irene and Jonathan Rogers.

Ledbury Hunt covering the grounds of the private house, Haffield, in Donnington. This is the front drive, where people are arriving for the meet. This was the Children's meet of 1964. On the right is Nimrod Champion, with the horse on the other side of the track being the whipper-in. *(Sheila Hitchon)*

The same hunt meet at Haffield. The horse on the right is the whipper-in, who assists the huntsman in managing the hounds. *(Sheila Hitchon)*

Nimrod Champion outside the front of Haffield, with his son Richard. Unfortunately Richard passed away in early 2008. *(Sheila Hitchon)*

The ladies here at Haffield, again in 1964, are Anne Windsor Clive, Lady Somers and Mrs A. Smith-Maxwell. Anne Windsor Clive was at this time retiring from the position of District Commissioner of the Ledbury Pony Club, which was then passed down to Mrs Smith-Maxwell. It is likely that Lady Somers presented the position from one lady to the other. *(Sheila Hitchon)*

Ledbury hounds at Haffield. Captain R. Hoare is on the far left and on the right is Mr E.F. Bensley, who were Joint Masters from 1963–66. Also at the front on the left is huntsman Nimrod Champion. *(Sheila Hitchon)*

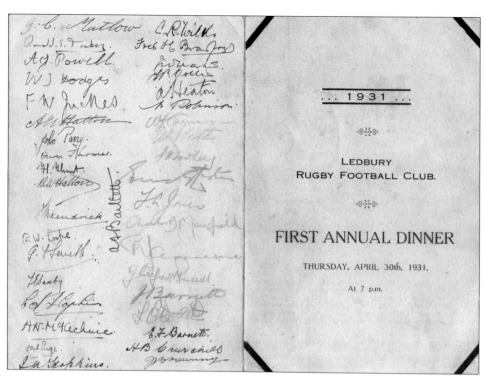

One of Ledbury's other main assets is the Ledbury Rugby Football Club. It has continued to increase its facilities and initiatives since it was founded in 1883. Its first annual dinner was held in April 1931. These two pictures show the dinner menu with the signatures of those who attended. *(John Wilesmith)*

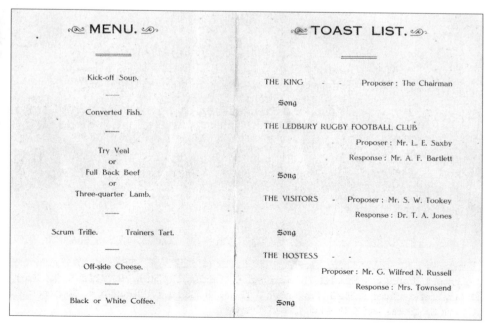

Playing rugby in the late 1940s, on the old ground near the railway. *(John Wilesmith)*

Ledbury first XV in 1986. The players in the back row are, from left to right: P. Houlbrooke, J. Cotton, J. Watkins, S. Brookes, R. Manning, R. Watkins, C. Cotton, M. Whittaker, P. Hunt, M. Leigh, and referee S. Black. Front row: D. Ewart, S. Green, J. Wilesmith, R. Chapman, C. Biggs, R. Kerr, S. Stevens and T. Weston. *(John Wilesmith)*

BIBLIOGRAPHY

BOOKS

Bishop, A., Murray, G. and Rowley, B., *Ledbury Street Names*, Logaston Press, 2007

Bick, D.E., *The Herefordshire & Gloucestershire Canal and the Gloucester – Ledbury Railway*, The Pound House, Newent, Glos, 1979

Eisel, J. and Shoesmith, R., *The pubs of Bromyard, Ledbury and east Herefordshire*, Logaston Press, 2003

Hillaby, J., *Ledbury: A Medieval Borough*, Logaston Press, 2005

Parr, F. *Notes of Old Ledbury*, 1884

Postle, D. *A Glimpse of Old Ledbury*, The Amadeus press Ltd, Huddersfield

Tilley's Illustrated Guide to Ledbury and District, Luke Tilley & Son

Ward, T. *Herefordshire's Postcard Past*, Logaston press, 2003

Ward, T. *The Archive photograph Series – Ledbury*, Chalfpord Publishing Co., 1996

Wargent, G. *Recollections of Ledbury*, 1905

Watkins, T.B. *The Ledbury Guide*, 1831; Hereford

Elizabethan Ledbury; Georgian Ledbury; Victorian & Modern Ledbury; all GHAL Local Books, 2007

WEBSITE

http://en.wikipedia.org/wiki/Border_Morris
(For the photograph at the bottom of page 114)